Cheers to You

Create a Life You Don't Need A Vacation From

Nathaniel Schooler

Disclaimer

The book is provided "as is", without warranty of any kind, expressed or implied including without limitations, accuracy, omissions, completeness or implied warranties or suitability or fitness for a particular purpose or other incidental damages arising out of the use or the inability to use the book. You acknowledge that the use of this service is entirely at your own risk. This Agreement is governed by English law. You acknowledge that you have read this Agreement and agree to be bound by its terms and conditions.

DEDICATION

This book is dedicated to my amazing daughter Maya.
My Dad, who is 87, helped to edit.
My Mum for believing in me when I needed it most.

CONTENTS

Contents

ACKNOWLEDGMENTS 6

Forward By...9

Bryan Eisenberg 9

NY Times Best Selling Author...9

Introduction 11

Personal Branding Is Now Table Stakes 13

Chapter 1. Preparing Brand You For Lift-Off............................16

There are many reasons to begin building your brand...........17

Trust yourself to be able to be who you want to be 18

A bit of my journey 18

The nature of your personal image is not set in stone 21

Pick a personal branding consultant carefully 22

How to Leverage Your Personal Brand....................................30

Self-branding and building your credibility will change your life..........31

You can build a personal brand no matter who you are 31

Chapter 2. Where Are You Now VS Where Would You Like To Be 34

Trust yourself to come up with the right strategies along the way 38

Where am I now? VS Where do I want to Be? How Do I get there? 40

Chapter 3. How To Define Your Brand 43

Pivoting your brand to move into a new career direction.......47

Chapter 4. How To Explain What You Do For Others 51

Explain what you do simply so people can understand 52

Chapter 5. How To Build Credibility And Authority.................................54

What have you done in the past that is remarkable?...............55

Chapter 6. Discovering What Makes You Different 59

Keep The Faith...60

Chapter 7. Discover Your Cornerstone Words..........................63

How you are perceived begins with words and then image...................63

Chapter 8. Crafting Your Image And Using Your Brand story board........66

Chapter 9. Social Media 69

Audit your social media profiles first.....................................69

Take the time to list all the taboo words and subjects 70

Make a list of the topics that you should talk about 70

Sharing corporate and owner generated content can be overdone..........71

Chapter 10. Marketing Yourself...72

There are many ways to show off brand you...........................72

Chapter 11. Brand Story Board Document.................................75

Chapter 12 - Create Your Perfect Day (Bonus resource) 77

One Last Thing...80

ABOUT THE AUTHOR..81

Resources 82

ACKNOWLEDGMENTS

Every small and painful step in self-development has been just a stepping stone to the life that I have created for myself now. This would not be possible without the support from my late soft sales coach Richard White and my first business coach Barry Joinson who put me through so much pain during my first ten sessions it changed me profoundly.

Thanks to the fast-growing team at Legacy Media Hub, Kim-Adele Randall, Nelly Shein, Juan Hoyos and Tanja Prokop for all their help and support and skills.

Thanks to my brother Jacques for the reality check and support. My sisters Heidi, Eve and Jessica across the pond for their encouragement and wise words.

Thanks to Bryan Eisenberg for his guidance and support in making this book a reality.

Thanks to Mike Briercliffe, and Douglas Commaille who have been instrumental in this journey.

Thanks to Sir John for all his assistance and on point advice over the years.

Thanks to Katarzyna, for pushing me to act and seeing the brilliance in me, when I missed it myself.

Thanks to Christina for all her help with graphics and an occasional reality check over the last five years.

My supportive friends· Yinga, Anet, Kathy, Donna, Louis, Shiona, Kate, Jim, Jamie, Charlie, Ehsan, Stu, James, Ed and Inga, Juan, Susanne, Lizzie, Steve, Amanda, Matt, Marco, Joseph, Tom, Elizabeth, Farah, Julia, Hamish and Alasdair.

Thanks to Will, Lesley, Rahul, Bhavna, Jonathan, Jason, Dan, Thomas, Eddie, Jocko, Jason & Erik, who have helped me to learn lots of new skills and lessons along the way.

Thanks to all the great guests and co-hosts on all our podcast shows and especially Michael Tobin OBE (who became a co-host for a few episodes and helped launch multiple shows), Nicolas Babin, Treasa Dovander & and the others who welcomed being interviewed and shared so much value with us.

Thanks to the fantastic IBM team for your warmth, hospitality and encouragement in particular from Harriet, Amber, Amy, Frank, Jennifer, Sarah, Raquel, Emily, Becky, Nereida and my fellow Futurists who have been supportive at every step of the way, Billee, Peter, John, Neil, Stephen, Angela, Bob and Brandon.

Thanks also to the incredible peeps at Oracle who helped me massively on my journey.

To the people that didn't give me the jobs I thought I wanted and used my entrepreneurial ideas and the clients who were slow to pay my invoices. You have all helped me get my life on track by building my determination, and I wish you every success.

I would love to mention everybody, but I would need another book to do so, so I would like to take this opportunity to thank everybody who has helped me on my journey of being successful—cheers to you ALL.

Forward By

Bryan Eisenberg

NY Times Best Selling Author

Four out of five people check their phones before brushing their teeth. Do you check email first? Facebook? How many of us are addicted to the little notification icons on our devices.

We live in a social world. As of 2016, 68% of all U.S. adults are Facebook users, while 28% use Instagram, 26% use Pinterest, 25% use LinkedIn and 21% use Twitter. As more and more people engage with social media it gets harder to stand out.

You aren't trying to be Instagram famous you tell me. You aren't looking to a YouTube star. That's ok, how many of you want to land a better job? Looking to find your significant other? Looking to connect with more people? Dive deeper into your passions and hobbies.

Today being social is a prerequisite. How many times in your life have you searched for someone on the interwebs just to find out a little more about them? If you haven't trust me your boss, college admission boards, potential date, etc. is on a mission to find out more about you with a couple of clicks on the screen.

What will they think about you? What will they be able to say you care about from looking at your profile?

Go ahead, search for me on Instagram, LinkedIn, Facebook, Twitter. Each one may look a bit different but it wouldn't take you long to figure out who I am. What I am passionate about and if I am the type of person you would want to spend time with. This is your personal brand. We all have one even if it is not public.

Many decisions are being made based on people learning about your personal brand. In fact, I would not own the house I do today if it wasn't that my personal brand was public. The previous owner was picky, wanted to know who he was selling to since the house was on a cul-de-sac. Even though there was 3 other similar offers on the house he chose us. Was I lucky or is their real value in boosting your personal brand online?

Nathaniel wants to help you get you boost your personal brand. Even if you are not sure what it is or what it looks like yet. But through these pages you should start to see the rise of the brand called "You."

Introduction

What Is Personal Branding, And Why Is It Important?

Personal branding, self-positioning, and all individual branding were first introduced in 1925 from The Law of Success by Napoleon Hill who studied the top Millionaires of his time. These ideas were expanded on his next book.

> *"It should be encouraging to know that practically all the great fortunes began in the form of compensation for personal services, or from the sale of IDEAS." Think and Grow Rich by Napoleon Hill (1937)*

The idea surfaced later in the 1981 book Positioning: The Battle for Your Mind, by Al Ries and Jack Trout.

Personal branding is a strategy for building your personal identity and making it known to the world. Personal branding is important because it helps you be seen as an individual who isn't just defined by their job title. It makes you more memorable, trustworthy, and valuable in any business or social situation.

Why Is Personal Branding Important?

You need to create your own personal profile. Your identity helps you to stand out. For example, Apple had used Steve Jobs personal branding much before he used it. Another well known personal brand is Elon Musk, but not in comparison. It would be reasonable if all entrepreneurs could develop relationships with potential customers first on an individual basis before delivering the company's message.

What Is Your Personal Brand?

Personal branding means something different to everyone; however, some commonalities make it successful: consistency with messaging across all communications is key. They are also building relationships online whilst being authentic.

Here's a personal branding forecast sure to intrigue you in the coming years:

The world is moving at an extremely high speed, and it'll take the self-proclaimed "fastest gun alive" to keep up. Think of how quickly things change today compared to 20 years ago. It's all about the growth mindset & coolness; staying current with what's trending.

According to Entrepreneur.com, when building a personal brand for business:

- 561% more reach from employees sharing messaging

- Content is shared 24X more frequently

- 8 X more engagement from employees VS brand

Branding has become more complex due to technology, the internet, and rapidly changing consumer trends. Therefore, understanding how to build a good profile will be crucial for your long-term success.

There'll be less emphasis on making a quick buck without putting time into building quality relationships. So that people know, like and trust you for the long term, developing yourself as a person with values, morals and passion – which are ultimately reflected in your brand will attract the right sort of people who want to do business with you.

It takes hard work and consistency to build, and there'll be many sleepless nights when you're trying to get things right. Build your persona authentically from the heart; it will pay off as you won't have to pretend to be a fake persona that you don't understand.

Personal Branding Is Now Table Stakes

If you as a professional don't have a budget to contribute personally to creating a personal brand, I suggest you discuss it with your H.R. department.

Quality will prevail. In the coming years, there'll be less emphasis on making a quick buck without putting time into building quality relationships; so that people know like and trust you for the long term. Developing yourself as a person with values, morals and passion – when you get it right, you will attract the right sort of people who will want to do business with you.

Building tangible value from someone's brand is not an easy task. It can differ in the metrics used to understand the value of your brand. However, when delivering personal brand projects, producing five figures or six figures on top of the bottom line for the business is not uncommon.

When leaving your current job, you have built up an asset value, combining your skills and your brand.

A personal brand is built day by day and takes a lot of effort. Every contact you make is a bi-product of that. The personal brand is creating an asset value and is a motivational tool to drive activities certainly for the salespeople.

There is a fear that can stop businesses from building their employees brands, and some people sit there with their expertise and telling people about their skills can assist the growth of revenue.

If you look to the future five years and think about where you would like to be in your life, you will find that those five years will pass very quickly. If you wish to move forwards towards the future and continue to be pushed around by your circumstance then probably don't continue to read this book. Probably just accept where you are right now and take the ambition that you have or had and forget all about your dreams and goals.

If you do want to stand out in a room full of similar professionals doing similar things then read on?

Learn how you show others what distinguishes your value from the pack.

How do you get them interested and keep their attention long enough to buy into your product or service?

This is not an easy task, but it doesn't have to be hard either.

Obtaining an understanding of what a personal brand is will set you up for success and this book represents almost 15 years of study into the subject by me and decades of experience from the mentors and coaches that I have had the privilege to work with over the last 10 years.

Very few understand "what a personal brand consists of?"; they think it is all about logos, photos and a website and blog posts. Yet, these elements are only a small part of the strategy and consistent authenticity that underpin your online self and how to market it.

So for now just forget all about pictures, logos and visuals, this book is for the people who want to get their words right.

Words are the precursor for ALL in this context.

Chapter 1. Preparing Brand You For Lift-Off

Taking control of how others perceive you is crucial to maximising opportunities in every area of your life. In this chapter we are going to give you a top level overview of what you will need to do to begin controlling how you show up in the world.

Like it or not, you have a personal brand, and if you give the wrong first impression, you may never know what you missed.

When people hire you, partner with you or even date you, they usually Google you first. Then they decide whether to invest valuable time in meeting you based upon what is written about you online.

You are always selling yourself to someone, and developing the correct wording to explain why you are the best person for the job.

If you are serious about wanting to stand out in your industry, win with your love life and be more successful in your career, then taking the time to build your brand is one of the best investments you will ever make.

You can build your brand at any stage

If you are reading this and longing for your next holiday or living for the weekend, then perhaps it is about time you took control of your career and stopped needing a vacation from your life.

The good news is you can begin to build your brand wherever you are in your career. So even if you don't like what you are doing for work right now or don't have a tremendous amount of time, you can still invest in your brand.

Often building your brand is a relentless battle between other people's opinions of what you should do, the faith in your abilities and taking the massive action steps needed to achieve success.

This is not another book about how easy it is to live the life of your dreams

It is not even a rag to riches story, nor a story about how effortless it is to achieve success; it contains a clear, simple methodology to build your brand story board and a little about the journey I took.

There are many reasons to begin building your brand

Whether you want to make more money, create more recognition for what you do, change jobs or even pivot your career into unchartered territories, building your brand is crucial to success.

If you trust yourself and build your brand the right way, you can earn a month's salary in one day, date the partner of your dreams and get the career recognition you deserve.

If you take control of your brand, you can create the life you want versus the life you inherited from your past decisions.

All the knowledge you need is at your fingertips to enable you to be anyone you want to be.

YOU are totally 'Unique', and the chances of you being born are Trillions to one. But, YOU are here for a reason, and this book will help you understand how to explain Your 'WHY' to the people who matter most.

Your brand evolves; a part of you contains a massive value if crafted correctly and not in haste. As a result, you can command more respect from your peers, make more money and have a more rewarding life. All you need to do is work on your brand, develop your skills, and trust yourself.

Trust yourself to be able to be who you want to be

Many of us have been told we can't do things or aren't good enough. Some of us have been told not to tell anyone how great we are as it is arrogant. Many remarkable people are waiting for their brilliance to be 'magically discovered' and for those people to tell the world.

The idea of waiting for things to fall into our laps is fundamentally wrong, of course, and unfortunately, it will not help us further our careers in our society.

It is doubtful that someone will discover you and tell anyone else unless you make it worthwhile for them to do so.

A bit of my journey

In the last 20 years, I have gone from working within premium retail, at my family's boutique winery, travelling the world, job hunting during the recession, and attending interviews after demoralising interviews for jobs that I didn't want.

All the interviews I went to were instrumental in my personal development and writing of this book.

One interview at a marketing company was like something from an advert for Carlsberg beer; I drove to Manchester, about 4 hours from where I lived. A gorgeous woman answered the door. The impressive office had a fridge full of beer and a pool table, and even more attractive women around. The people were lovely, but unfortunately, I didn't get the role.

Thanks to this magical moment, I decided that the world of marketing was where I wanted to be.

I then began my journey into marketing by learning how to use social media to arrange sales meetings to sell beer and then brand consultancy. Shortly after this pivotal moment in my career, I began to build my brand and to lead social media and marketing workshops for small businesses until I was hired to coach marketing workshops for Microsoft and IBM.

Subsequently, I was invited to write for IBM, which was a massive milestone in my career considering how I could not write anything vaguely interesting until I reached 35.

My English teacher had put me off writing for 20 years, and I was not too fond of his classes as they were so dull. We would misbehave and laugh and joke around, and he would regularly say- *"You'll be cleaning bloody toilets boy!"* by today's standards, this is, of course, child abuse; I digress…

In my mid 30's I discovered a book by Seth Godin called 'The Icarus Deception', which gave me the confidence to begin writing despite my lack of immediate skill. I trusted myself, and writing became an excellent outlet for my stress and freedom for my mind.

Whatever your reasons are for learning more about personal branding, if you trust yourself to follow the advice in this book, you can begin to build your brand and develop the skills needed to take your career to the next level.

No matter where you are in your career, you can always move forwards. Taking the time to be conscious of how you look, what you say and how others perceive you is critical to showing off your skills in the right light.

This book will enable you to begin building your brand, there is no fluff, and there are very few examples of people to borrow words from as it focuses on your uniqueness.

Before we dig into the details, I will clear up some myths around personal branding

It does not start with a photo, a logo or your physical appearance; it starts with you and your intent and wording:

It starts with intent! What do you want to achieve?

What do you want to be recognised for?

What do you want to do with your career?

Which direction do you want to head?

Who is your audience?

Who will be your prospective clients?

Taking the time to think about what you want to do with your career and tell your story are crucial elements.

Researching other people you respect in other industries and the industry you are in is a good idea. So what can you do to self-brand and build professional success?

You may not even want to be visible online as you don't need to use it to make money, although whether you like it or not, you still have a brand you!

Online presence does not equal personal branding:

Keep in mind it is up to you to decide how you show up in the world, what story are you telling. All people on the internet and in the world are not equal.

You can certainly earn millions of dollars over your lifetime more than someone who is in the exact same role as you, just because you take the right action where it matters.

Or do you just want to opt-out from the internet altogether?

If you are a very private person, you may not wish to share your entire life online; if you decide you want to be a public figure or industry influencer, then perhaps you will require a beautifully designed YouTube channel and your own site to show off your best self.

You could be a solicitor, accountant or busy CEO and not wish to spend loads of time engaging with people. So brand-you needs to be designed accordingly…if you establish yourself as a thought leader, blogger and someone who lives and breathes social, you may want to have a VA because people will engage with you.

The nature of your personal image is not set in stone

How do you define your audience?

How many social media accounts should I have?

What kind of content will I share on each platform?

Will my visuals show me as being funny, quirky or serious?

Does my profile make it clear what the readers can expect from me? What's my 30-second pitch (the most compelling sentence that describes what you do)? How do I describe myself without bragging to impress potential clients/customers and industry peers?

People must know you, (not necessarily) like you, however, they must trust you.

Although people will still see you and follow you along your journey online, they do not know you as a person. It's like sitting in the stands at a football game; whilst you can see everything happening on the pitch, it does not make you a part of the team. Likewise, people don't associate with strangers but yourself with other businesses and leaders in your industry.

Personal branding is all about defining what kind of person you are and then communicating that message to the appropriate audience who needs to hear it!

What steps should I take when building my personal brand? Here's what I recommend:

Before putting together your blueprint document, it is necessary to start some research, and once you do your research you will see many ways people suggest you do it.

If you do not enjoy writing, I recommend you ask a friend to help you. Or you can always choose a strategy consultant who will have some personal branding examples to show you from prior client work.

Pick a personal branding consultant carefully

Some personal branding consultants suggest their (untested or badly thought out) ways to build your online presence, they have no experience and no tangible process or testimonials.

When/if looking for someone to help you with your "individual branding" to build credibility, I would recommend using someone who has over a decade of experience in this business.

Personal brands are becoming ubiquitous and are something that overzealous marketers seem to think are also experts in creating them.

While maybe something they can and do offer as a service, most of them will not be able to show you any examples, as they have never worked with someone like you. And you are perfectly capable to begin to create your own with a little help from this book.

Pay attention: these are the questions to ask, as there are many different consultants:

How long have they been doing personal branding?

Where did they learn their process?

Who have they worked with?

Can you speak to them?

Will they offer you a money-back guarantee?

Then the questions will be more specific:

Have you worked with top influencers?

Do you specialise in self-branding and online presence?

What industries do you specialise in?

Do you have a strong personal brand yourself?

Have you helped anyone else build a personal brand that has had an impact on their target audience?

You need to know the answer to these questions before hiring someone to help with your self-branding and help create a personal brand; whilst it is not rocket science the competition has increased in the past 5 years, and everyone thinks they can do it.

Personal branding strategy and your goals must align and it is recommended that when you approach something as important as this, you have a specific purpose and goals.

Do you want to create your value proposition?

Do you want an online presence and an effective personal brand?

Do you want to create a personal website?

Do you want to be a leader in your industry?

Do you want to create your personal media platforms?

Do you want to build an online reputation through your personal website?

This will help keep you more focused on what needs to be done and how best to achieve it.

Having no real plan of direction gives you very little chance of achieving a positive outcome for your life and business.

1) Start with research: when I ask people about themselves, they say "I don't know" or "my friends, family & clients know me as..."

In my experience, this is never the case as everyone knows exactly who they are, but not many can articulate those thoughts into something recognised by others as value.

So if you're reading this book and haven't put your personal branding strategy together, I would take the time to digest this book and then follow the processes in the following chapters.

2) Now, list all the things you like about the people you have researched and what they say or do online that make you like them.

With this exercise, YOU get to decide what you will be like moving forwards and not what others want you to be like!

The best way is to begin to build a draft of your blueprint document; if you have no idea, start with the question, "what do I want my audience to think about me when they hear or see my name?" This may seem like a simple question, but it will help guide you in the right direction. By asking yourself this question, it will also make it easier for you to plan how and where exactly you want to show up in the world; if it were easy, everyone would do it successfully!

Building a blueprint document will really help

A blueprint document will save you a lot of time when putting together your CV or Resume. It also saves you a lot of time deciding what to write about yourself on your website and social profiles.

Having a process to make you stand out is key

Your process is based on your intent. Therefore, it is important to clarify your expectations and goals and the important things before you start. This helps ensure that you reinforce those qualities with everything else you do, and what you want to do in your specific niche or new direction should come easy.

– The world is moving at an extremely high speed, and it'll take YOU, the self-proclaimed "EXPERT", to keep up. It's all about the credibility and the company that you keep, especially on social media.

– Understanding how to build your own profile will be crucial for your long term success and providing you stay on track and enjoy what you are doing will be fun too!

– There's less emphasis on making a quick buck and now more about lifelong relationships that support you and your community.

How do I brand myself personally?

Starting with a blueprint document, you begin to put your current words or want to be known for. The document contains the four key elements of building a brand blueprint and acts as a precursor to creating any content:

What are your keywords?

What do you do or want to do?

Why are you better and or different?

What gives you authority and credibility?

Once you have begun compiling this document and looking at the people you look up to, you will begin to have something useful for your own personal PR activities. These personal PR activities include but are not limited to:

- Elevator pitch
- Resume or CV
- LinkedIn profile
- Twitter profile
- Website bio
- Author page
- Magazine or TV intro
- Podcast introduction

Once you have your blueprint you will have easy, consistent

communications across all your channels

PR stands for "public relations." So, this is really building relationships with the people you want to work with, and I think working with you will be mutually beneficial.

– Personal branding should build awareness for your business and elevate it above competitors by creating credibility and authority.

– You can do this by working on a project and maintaining consistent communications within a niche or industry.

A benefit of PR is that professionals in marketing and corporate social responsibility are often using PR tactics to gain exposure for their products or services.

For example: companies pay publicists to develop press releases about new products, sponsor coverage of an event, or create content for strategic media placements like news stories, video segments, interviews, blog posts… etc.

Your profile is your online identity. This means that the way you behave on social media or craft your email signature should have a consistent feel. For example, if you want to be perceived as an expert, speak like one; when you craft emails, make sure they are compelling and use proper grammar, spelling and punctuation.

Remember it doesn't stop here, so you can check out the blog on LegacyMediaHub.Com on domains and having your own personal domain instead of a Gmail address! It is called 11 Reasons To Use Your Own Domain Name and is listed in the resources section.

You already have an audience

Knowledge is power, and so are words

People will look up to people who are one or two steps ahead

Creating your profile should be easier than ever before with today's technology:

Although with all these people making noise, you need to craft your wording and your four key elements very carefully and be consistent. Once you have decided what you want to be known for and written your communications brand blueprint, it will be time to move forward.

Keep your hopes, dreams, promises, and intentions front of mind as you craft your story; people will look up to people who are one or two steps ahead.

Personal Brand For Business

Your personal brand is what you do, how you do it, and why. To trust your business, customers need to trust you first!

Marketing yourself as a professional or self-branded to make sure your self-brand stands out from the pack. It doesn't mean you are someone else; it just means you create a personal brand for things you want to be known for.

Where are you trying to go starts before building A personal brand!

- You may not think you need a personal brand until you sell your business or need a new job
- Get headhunted because your personal brand is great and you are great at what you do
- Building your business up or your career follows your personal brand
- Pivoting your career and using your brand to do that

If you don't know what your personal brand is how can you sell yourself, you need to be in control of your career path

You have a personal brand like it or not so don't neglect it

Your personal brand is what you do, how you do it, and why.

But first, your personal brand needs to be baked into all aspects of the business: from marketing, logos and websites, to packing materials and customer service strategy. And if done right? Your corporation will benefit hugely!

First things first, though – what is a personal brand for business anyway? It's marketing yourself as a professional or self-branded to make sure your self-brand stands out from the pack. Marketing departments can certainly assist here, at least when writing blogs and social media; some marketing people understand branding, and some marketing people don't!

Successful businesses are looking for people that align with their values, so they know they'll stay invested in their customers' success long term. With your own authentic voice at the helm (and not someone else telling them who to be), prospects will see the true colours, whatever marketing efforts are deployed.

Personal branding begins with research and consists of some or all of these steps:

- Marketing research
- Look at personal brand examples
- Brand blueprint creation once researched
- Sharpening your physical appearance if applicable
- Getting a professional photo for profiles
- Personal website research and design

- Marketing with articles, blog post(s), guest blog(s),
- Write a new Twitter bio, LinkedIn profile, CV/Resume
- Grow social networks and target your desired audience
- Use social media tools to share content and build further
- Get interviews on podcasts and television or webinars
- Get interviews on Youtube channels (s) or television
- Build a Youtube channel or build a podcast show
- Write a book that is focused on pain of your audience

In this book we dig into more details for the important things to focus on when personal branding yourself for work:

When you look at the industry you are in or wish to enter, the personal brands you see can often be intimidating, especially if you enter a new industry or new role.

Don't be intimidated, everyone has to start somewhere.

How to Leverage Your Personal Brand

To Create Your Authentic Personal Brand for Success takes time and Effort!?

Wherever you are here in your career, understanding that building a successful personal brand is now not just important; it is critical to be taken seriously by recruiters and by the market or industry you and your executive leadership team.

People want to work with someone they know, like, and trust, although the like bit isn't necessarily needed for people to work with you.

You build your target audience based on your content and attitude, your professional success and showing up as your best self help you tell your story and build friends and connections who know, like and trust you.

As you define your audience, keep in mind that some prospective clients will be watching you from afar; you may not even know that they are there.

You could hire a PR firm or freelance writer to build your presence

To build a strong brand, you can either hire a PR firm or a freelance writer to build your online presence, and many different opportunities exist to get going with self-promotion. Guest posts, writing a blog post for your LinkedIn profile.

Self-branding and building your credibility will change your life

Once you begin to build credibility, you will transform your professional life for the better! People will begin to pay attention to you; they will notice when you have become a public figure; your written content, elevator pitch, and "top influencer" status may push you slightly out of your comfort zone.

You can build a personal brand no matter who you are

Whether you are a graphic designer in New York, a dentist in Hereford, or a technology firm's CEO. When your name shows up in the search results on LinkedIn or Google, and a beautifully designed brand such as yours shows up amongst the other top influencers is the time when you will realise it was worth investing the time and effort in creating yours.

When you build a personal brand, your career may take a new direction; you may want to obtain a better job or get a new job or even create a new career trajectory.

Then set up your website or blog and social channels.

After you have crafted your personal brand blueprint, you should start by setting up a website and make sure to create content, perhaps include Youtube videos or get your Instagram account or your own website site where you can really showcase the key points you want to make about the expertise in your specific niche.

This brings us to social media, which can help you make personal connections and build your brand online by putting out valuable content that is authentic to the real you.

To keep me from procrastinating, I make sure to interact with interesting people. There are lots of cool people on IM that I can talk to. In addition, Twitter and Facebook are great places to find people who share the same interests as me.

Having a thought leadership strategy for corporate leaders is one of the most powerful ways to build your business if you are not sure how, please read some of my other articles on my website.

Preparing your personal branding for success involves interacting with important people in your industry who are doing interesting things to get started on your quest for thought-leadership status.

I like Facebook and Twitter, but I think that LinkedIn is the best social media for work. If you are not sure about this or anything else related online, please read some of my other articles on my website to help you achieve your goals faster than you ever imagined possible!

Once you have a target audience, like any brand, you'll want to keep them engaged. That can be accomplished by including videos on blogs, webinars or useful educational information pieces.

Personal branding is a chance for you to flex your creative muscles, so have fun with it as this is like playtime for grown adults!

I have loads of other articles and free resources around this important topic, which I'll be linking to this article in the coming weeks.

If you are not sure how to get started or exactly what steps to take in the process of building a personal brand for success, then please read on. In this book we dig into more details for the important things to focus on when personal branding yourself for work.

Chapter 2. Where Are You Now VS Where Would You Like To Be

Before you begin to think about building your brand, it is crucial to take the time to decide where you want to be.

You can make the most of your opportunities in life and create the life you want. You need to trust yourself and have a plan.

Knowing where you want to go in your car is key to keeping you from burning all your fuel driving around with no direction.

If you are utterly miserable at work and are living for your vacation time, do not worry, there will be skills you are learning that will be valuable for finding the type of work you love.

Sometimes your life may fall to pieces before you can rebuild it

I was miserable, I was working all the hours that I could squeeze in between doing childcare; exercising, drinking, and womanising seemed like my only escape.

I had just left my wife and moved in with a friend of mine called Stu, and it was a bit like Joey and Chandler from an episode of friends, and we used to watch movies, drink beer, and laugh a lot.

If you are stuck, then ask for help and fast

Thankfully, before total self-destruction set in, a friend of mine introduced me to a business coach called Barry to get my life on track.

If you are anything like me, you put a brave face on and try to be happy, getting as much fulfilment and enjoyment from the things that you enjoy so you can ignore your problems and pretend that everything is alright.

Before building a personal brand working out what you want is crucial. When I met Barry, I had no idea what I wanted, and I was swamped managing social media for my clients, writing content and managing LinkedIn groups.

I booked up a 10-week coaching course, and every week without fail, Barry helped me understand the pain or lack of activity; that was in many cases holding me back from the actions that would get me to the place of creating a life I didn't need a vacation from.

It was emotional. The pain he put me through every week was unbelievable. Although looking back on it now, I didn't realise how unhappy I was at the time and the emotional baggage I had been carrying around. But, like I said, *"I put a brave face on and made the most of it."*

It was a cathartic process working out what I wanted and putting it down on paper.

Over the ten weeks, I realised that my life was entirely out of balance and the only way to get it in shape was to firstly work out where I wanted to go, which elements were out of balance and then, of course, to act.

Generally, nothing works in life unless you do! Sure, sometimes things are easy, but generally, that is just because you enjoy what you are doing and have honed your skills.

Since writing the first edition of this book, life has changed. I have started a business and had much more coaching this time from Kim-Adele and Nelly Shein, both of which have helped me tremendously to get my life on track. However, I strongly advise you to speak with a coach if you are stuck. Building your brand may not be the best option for you at this time.

Your journey all starts with awareness, where are you VS where you want to go

The most important thing is knowing where you want to go, not wallowing in the pain of where you are now. The more you focus on where you are now and the things you are unhappy about, the more your brain will look for something to be disappointed and dissatisfied with and continue the cycle of unhappiness.

The more we focus on things, the more they expand, and if you take the time to think about where you would like to be, you will be able to focus on creating a plan.

When I began building my brand, I found it quite daunting and looking back. I wish that I had taken the time to decide where I wanted to go much sooner.

Take the time to think about how happy you are at work

There are many different criteria for analysing where you are in your career. First, of course, there are the monetary ones, and there are the time constraints, the recognition, and the overall happiness goals. But, most importantly, you must be honest with yourself. So, for example, if you are delighted at work, you can build the wording you need to show off your key attributes.

If you are not happy at work and have not created the life you want yet, then you must begin to trust yourself and the process of self-realisation you are going through.

All your experiences have made you the individual that you are today

Going to interviews can certainly mess up your self-esteem, and you can begin to doubt your skills. Sometimes you have to stop all activities and think about where you want to go. This may seem like the worst advice if you are desperate for money, but it is the only way to take control of your career; it is a bit like when you are lost in your car and decide to drive around aimlessly with no knowledge of where you are.

Luckily for me, I realised that I wanted to get into marketing, and the failed interviews I went to are now just fun times in my life to look back on.

"Failure is a big part of success" Mike Tobin OBE Technology Entrepreneur

I got sick of recruiters using sales techniques to persuade me to attend interviews to promise a great job a brand-new Mercedes, pension, healthcare, etc. Then when I left, they never spoke to me again; sick of the endless miles I drove with PowerPoint decks that took me two days to create and the expense of printing them for someone to tell me that I was too senior for the job.

The desperation can set in like poison, the worry about not being able to afford to eat, the stress our spouse puts us under to pay for the next holiday or other things they want. Instead, use these bad experiences to help catapult you to new levels of success.

Things happen for a good reason, though it may not be apparent at the time

We may think that the job opportunity we have in front of us is what we want, but it could cause us to be in a worse position, a bit like the ridiculous interview I went to with a professional con artist.

Let me tell you the story.

One of my best friends, Louis got me a job interview in London at a company selling investments, the CEO interviewed me personally, and he took great pleasure in saying, *"You look like shit!" So* I went home and looked in the mirror and remember thinking he was right, so I vowed to look after my skin after that.

It turned out he was a con artist who made a lot of money selling fake Jatropha oil to would-be investors and went on the run from the cops after emptying the bank account and never paying any of the 60+ members of the telesales team!

Sometimes in life, we are meant to stop and smell the coffee

Taking the time to revisit where I wanted to go has started to pay dividends. I spent a considerable amount of time deciding what I loved to do VS what had to be done, and this came with a realisation that I loved to write.

Despite the encouragement from friends and family to get a full-time job making sales, I am still very skilled from back when I used to sell wine. So I decided to stick to my guns and now get paid to write, create content and help people with their brands and marketing.

Last month I was asked to write two blogs and record a video, and I am now paid more money than I used to earn in a month in one day.

Creating a life, you don't need a vacation from

Taking the time to think about what a perfect day for you at work may sound incredibly corny, but it should be something you give some thought to; integrating your career into your life and creating a balanced life is certainly something to strive for.

Often some elements of your life will cross over. For example, obtaining balance is something you can achieve in some instances, but usually, if you don't plan, certain aspects will disappoint you or cause you stress.

Making your work and life co-exist are the critical elements to a happy life. Working out what your perfect day looks like should be your top priority. List all the key elements of that day and put a plan together for where you want to be.

Trust yourself to come up with the right strategies along the way

The good news is your brand plan is not like that. You can come up with an objective, and if you follow specific steps to become more visible and build more authority and credibility and, of course, act, you will be able to hit your objective despite your strategy changing along the way.

The perfect day for me is waking up at 5, or 6 am, exercising for an hour or two and then getting stuck into reading the news, then writing articles and inviting new guests onto one of our podcast shows.

A perfect day for you may be driving to work and then spending time in meetings with clients; it all depends on what you love to do and how you want to live.

Some people want to work for a corporation, and others want to work for themselves. You should consider this; do you want to leave the certainty of a regular paycheck to chase the entrepreneurial dream, or are you happy working for a business?

You will still have to do things at work that you don't like, but the more you realise what you do want, the more you will excel in these areas. If you build your brand around things you love, a new job may come along; an opportunity to partner with someone who loves to do the jobs you hate may arrive or an opportunity to reduce the time doing the things you hate.

If you don't work out what you like and don't like, how do you expect to build more of the life you want?

Now take the time to list all the things you enjoy doing and list the topics you would like to learn more about that you could make money from. Focusing on what you want and taking the time to learn more is a sure-fire way to have a more rewarding career and to make money from the things you love to do.

Following the formula on the next few pages is a great place to start

This helps you remove the stress from deciding and alleviates the risk of you following your emotions. It is good to have all your thoughts on a piece of paper versus in your head, where they can drive you to distraction. You can review this every few months for progress and update it accordingly.

Where am I now? VS Where do I want to Be? How Do I get there?

What Is My Position Today?	What Do I Want To Achieve?	How Do I Achieve It?
My Secret Ambitions		
My Training **What do I expect from my training?**		
My Physical Condition **What can I do to** **improve my physical condition?**		
My Job **How can I develop my job so that it**		

What Is My Position Today?	What Do I Want To Achieve?	How Do I Achieve It?
will become more satisfying?		
Home Is it the oasis I want it to be?		
My External Activities Do I want to travel more?		
My Financial Position Do I draw up budgets?		
My Other Activities On what essential things will I spend my resources?		

*My father used this table to teach 2500+ postgraduate students how to be effective executives and keep track of their ambitions spanning a career of 17+ years of teaching and winning the J.P. Morgan Award for assisting MIT for over 45 years.

Of course, taking the time to list what is crucial for you is key to creating the life you want. Then create a diagram like the one below and start to put in the goals you want to achieve.

My first business coach Barry Joinson took the time to go through with me my goals and the areas of life I was unhappy with and happy about and now I have made massive progress to the new goals I set a few years ago.

Trust yourself and find your focus

Once you are definite about what you do and you manage to understand what you do best, you will be able to focus on the things that make you tick, the things that make you want to jump in the air and scream at the top of your lungs because you love what you are doing. My dad put it very well. The other day he said just, "what do you do really well?"

So now you need to read the rest of this book and trust yourself to carefully craft your wording so you can explain to others why they should buy into you.

If you are keen to build your brand, please do email me
nat@natschooler.com

Chapter 3. How To Define Your Brand

Explaining what you do precisely in words that everyone can understand is not that easy until you shift your mindset. Unfortunately, very few people understand technical terminology and using the wrong language is costing you dearly in lost revenue.

People think that using complicated words is necessary to make themselves sound more critical. They believe that these words give extra weight when they speak. However, most of the time, including them, is a waste of words as they mean nothing and confuse people.

On many occasions, C-level executives, entrepreneurs and others are too busy to find the time needed to build their brands. As a result, they waste considerable time on social media without reaping any rewards; they have no credibility or authority in their marketplace. Unfortunately, they talk about what they do in words no one understands, so no one takes them seriously.

Often, they just need a little guidance to get their wording right or use a thesaurus before building their brand and growing their visibility. This helps develop their careers and businesses the right way without being seen as aloof or unapproachable.

Unfortunately, some still jump onto social media without formulating the suitable wording first to express who they are in the right way. Usually, a considerable amount of money is wasted without even having the basics in place first. Many have no experience or understanding of the first steps needed to build a brand or the time-honoured processes that should be used to get the best results.

The valuable time wasted on social media would be better off working out the correct wording to show their key elements. Using simple words that a 12-year-old child can understand pays dividends.

Just imagine if you were asked what you do for a living by someone that had no idea about the industry buzzwords, but they owned a company, or their family owned a huge company, and you explained in your technical wording what you did. You would stop them from doing business with you or introducing you to their team for that job offer you were looking for.

Trust yourself: don't copy other people's wording

Some, unfortunately copy other people's wording because they either think they lack the skills, the time, or the eloquence to put together a brand story board themselves.

If you do copy others, it can make you seem untrustworthy in an interview or a meeting, as you will not come across as genuine and in most cases, you won't remember to use the words in your resume, on your website or in your LinkedIn profile. You may not have the knowledge to back up what you are saying.

Following a straightforward process for putting the brand, a blueprint is essential. This process helped me, and many of our clients have the sort of profiles that engage and inform. So people understand what they are all about and in a tone that works for their target audience. So naturally, this has led to stronger relationships and better network growth and has helped grow their businesses and relationships.

Some build personal brands quickly and begin to obtain the recognition they deserve for their inner genius very fast. Many rapidly gain recognition for their skills when they get the All-important wording right and promote themselves authentically.

Trust yourself to use simplicity

Before you begin, I recommend you find a Thesaurus and think of some friends, family, or colleagues you can ask to give you some feedback. Ideally, it would be best to work with a colleague or friend to get your wording right and get rolling on your journey. Doing the simple exercises in this book with someone else is very helpful to refine your language.

Embrace your uniqueness and tell the world why you

Whether you are just starting in your career, working towards getting a better job or building your own business, investing in your brand is one of the most important things that you will ever do.

If you do not take control, then you are at the mercy of Google and other websites, which retain your information for many years; your digital footprint is out there whether you like it or not. So taking the time to manage it and show off your skills in the right light is one of the best things you can do to attain the career recognition you need and safeguard your future success.

No matter where you are from or what job you do, building your brand will enable you to create a better career and have a more rewarding life.

Trusting yourself and sharing your unique voice without being afraid to stand up and be counted is one of the best things I have ever done in my professional career and is why I help others to do the same.

Don't forget your personality and opinions may not suit everyone's taste

So, take the time to consider who you are and who you would like to work with. Then make sure that you show this off in the right light by using the right words.

Do not become just another carbon copy of someone you have seen online who you think looks good. Instead, trust yourself and don't be afraid to be authentic, move forward, and grow into the person you would like to be and, in many cases, already are.

You have invested in learning skills, now tell the world what they are

Building my brand is one of the best investments I have ever made, and whilst at first, it was not easy, it gave me a sense of focus and a certain degree of professionalism that is expected in this competitive world.

No matter what industry you are in, you will find people who have worked at making their brands stand out, and they will be using their brand to build whichever business they are working with and building its brand alongside their brand and visa-versa.

Completely authentic people have built the most successful personal brands throughout history. This is because they defined clearly what they do, why they do it differently, and who they do it for. These are just some of the critical elements in building one's brand, which I explain in more detail throughout this book.

Throughout history, what you do and what you leave behind can be seen to be part of your brand. So many people reading this will be thinking, but I am not Nelson Mandela or Mother Theresa; remember, you still need to think about your brand if you want to create more success within your professional life. Trust yourself. You are more capable than you realise, and the magic happens when you push yourself.

Take the time to get your wording right and review it

Many business owners, entrepreneurs, and C-level executives I speak to understand a personal brand but have left out many vital elements. Some manage to show off their brand in the right light successfully and need a few tweaks and an objective opinion to improve their work. Others need to take the time to get their wording right and to be able to describe what they do to their target markets, what gives them authority and credibility and why they are different and better than anyone else.

Lots of entrepreneurs and business professionals get distracted by their day-to-day tasks; they get immersed inside the business and forget all about their brands instead of working on moulding them to show off their skills and attributes in the right way.

Trust yourself: take the initiative to build your brand

Whether you want to make more money, create more recognition for what you do, change jobs, or even pivot your career into unchartered territory, your brand can help you.

Your brand is something that evolves, and it is a part of you that contains a massive value if crafted correctly and not in haste.

Many of us have been told we can't do things or aren't good enough; many have been told we shouldn't be arrogant or tell anyone how good they are. So, many people are waiting for their brilliance to be magically discovered and for others to tell the world.

Trust yourself: tell your story, and others will too

The idea of waiting for things to fall into our laps is fundamentally wrong, of course, and unfortunately, it is not going to help us further our careers in our society. It is doubtful that someone will discover us and tell anyone else unless we make it easy for them to do so.

Pivoting your brand to move into a new career direction

Personal branding was something I didn't give any thought to myself until about five years after I left my father's business. I had built authority and credibility in the wine industry as we had an excellent brand for nearly 25 years.

It may seem simple, but without the right guidance and breaking it down into manageable steps, brand marketing and the storytelling that goes with it are time-consuming and costly.

It can be steered in the right direction, providing you take the time to create a bridge between where you are now and where you want to be heading. You can use your past as an advantage; in fact, your past is one of the critical elements of your brand, so why not invest the time in yourself for maximum results.

Many people don't make the time, and they don't have the eloquence or the skills to create their brand story board. The good news is you can begin with as little or as much time as you have. The words you use can be chopped and changed if you take enough time to use a thesaurus.

Many businesses now contribute towards personal branding coaching. Many will even pay for someone to help you find the right words to describe what you do and for good profile shots and perhaps a promotional video depending on your role within the business.

In many cases creating a few short statements tailored to your target audience is the most challenging task. Unfortunately, getting started seems the biggest hurdle, like anything new in life. Usually, employers and business owners spend ages trying to get these words right. They don't do anything and believe that their business brand is enough to grow their sales when their employees and senior management teams don't have up-to-date profiles on their social networks.

The good news

Once the first statements are complete, you will feel a lot better about building your brand, and you will begin to enjoy the process of positioning yourself.

You can then use some of the statements for your social media profiles, and obviously, the/your website and resume can contain all your relevant information.

The brand story board is a core block of wording with no fluff, word waste, and grammar or punctuation. Once it is in place, it acts as a word palette for writing articles. When writing press releases, you or your P.R. or agency partners can also use these words.

In the next chapter, we cover some more key elements of your brand and look forward to helping you understand more about what you need to do to make your brand stand out in front of the crowd.

Follow the process outlined to create your brand story board

I have taken the time to make this process as simple as possible for you to build your brand statements. They will formulate part of your brand story board for use in your CV or Resume (as they call it in the states) and, of course, for use on your all-important social media profiles and any other marketing materials you have or decide to create in the future.

You can be selective as to how you use the words in different publications to appeal to the audience's demographics.

Creating your wording should not be complicated; however, it takes some brainpower, and I recommend you take regular breaks, go for a walk, go to the gym, or have a nap.

Writing about what you do may take a few revisions, and having a personal brand partner or friend bounce ideas off is helpful.

Create your statements in the fewest words possible; grammar is not something to worry about here. You can add in punctuation as you utilise the statements. The brand story board is a basic structure, so you can use it a bit like a colour palette if you are painting.

I recommend compiling all the statements into the book's last page so you have your brand story board in one place.

Whatever your reasons are for learning more about personal branding, you can understand the process I used to define my brand, and if you follow the advice, you can also build your brand and take control of your career.

Chapter 4. How To Explain What You Do For Others

I will assume you have a clear idea of what you do for others or want to do, I will also assume you have a thesaurus that you can use, and you have the time to invest in thinking about the best words to put into your benefit-led statements.

Take ownership of your success and show others fast

Explaining how we can help others very simply so they can understand well enough to tell other people what we do is crucial.

Using the correct wording to describe what you do will pay dividends, especially when it comes to people introducing you to others. If you cannot explain what you do to others, how are they supposed to understand what you do first and then introduce you to others?

Could you keep it simple stupid?

Being able to explain what you do for others in simple words that a 12-year-old can understand is key to getting your brand out there to as many people as possible. This way, when people talk about you, they market your skills for you, instead of saying statements like *'he is in computers'* or 'he *'is a recruiter',* these explanations do you no favours at all and will end up costing you dearly.

Never forget people do business with you because they 'know', 'like' (ideally) and most importantly 'trust you'.

It takes time for people to get to know you, and indeed being able to explain what you do in simple words that everyone understands is crucial to the first stage in crafting your brand story board.

We begin with listing a few key statements of what you do for others. For example, If you are a personal assistant, you could say -

"I help executives get organised to make time for the urgent and important."

If you are a marketer -

"I help businesses get better results from their marketing campaigns."

'Take the headache away from managing paid ads'

'Reduce the costs of marketing campaign delivery.'

'Design the best customer experiences.'

'Create cost savings through buying the right ad space.'

These statements clearly define the benefits you provide and should not be rushed.

Taking the time to build this foundational wording is crucial to the success of your brand, I was speaking to a very successful businessman who said to me, *'keep it simple stupid'*.

Explain what you do simply so people can understand

You need to be able to explain what you have to offer and why people should know, like and trust you. Being resilient in honing your skills and presenting them to the people who matter is vital.

Harvard marketing professor Theodore Levitt:

"People don't want to buy a quarter-inch drill. They want a quarter-inch hole."

Take the time to think about these benefit-led statements carefully and remember that punctuation does not exist here and the fewer words you use, the better.

List 5 Benefit Led Statements About What You Do For Others

Ok, so now you have listed these statements, you need to think about them. Take the time to revisit this tomorrow and see if you can add any value.

The rest of this book contains a straightforward process you can follow, but it is not an instant fix. Building your brand takes time, and anyone who promises you an instant personal brand is obviously like a used car salesman selling you a headache that someone else needs to fix.

When building your brand, following a transparent process is crucial to success, and I have stripped down all the key elements to explain what you do to the people who matter in words they understand.

Take the time to think and mull over your wording in your mind for a few days. If you rush it the words will not only not feel right to you when you read them, but they will not show you off in the right light.

Chapter 5. How To Build Credibility And Authority

Remember, people do business with you when they know, like and trust you, although sometimes they don't have to like you if you are great at what you do, although it does make for smoother relationships when they do like you.

Being credible is essential for people to trust you and your abilities. Staying focused on what you do best and sticking to this is vital; consistency is gained by repeating what you do and delivering the best possible outcome.

Overpromise and under deliver at your peril

Credibility is built in many ways. The most important one is to under-promise and over-deliver. This is the way to continue maintaining high-quality work and build credibility. But, again, delighting your customer and co-workers is vital.

Being known for doing a great job consistently will pay dividends when people want to find someone who delivers, having a smile on your face and being nice to deal with also help but the main thing is quality work.

To be trusted is the most crucial part of building your credibility, once you have begun to build trust you will see the rewards, people will want to do business with you as you are seen to be the go-to person or company within your space.

The trust element helps businesses to grow incrementally because you are seen to be at the forefront in your industry, you work hard to stay up to date with the latest information and take the time to build your knowledge on a daily basis.

At the time of writing the first version of this book I was an official IBM Futurist which gave me instant credibility as they are one of the top 10 brands in the world and would not invite me into their community if I wasn't knowledgeable in my space.

Being credible is also something that can be affected by who you work with, imagine if you got a job with Anthony Robbins or Oprah Winfrey and they gave you a testimonial, they say it's who you know and not what you know and, in some cases, this is still true.

Always be educating yourself to stay one step ahead

If you are going to be trusted you always need to be educating yourself and be better than yesterday, striving to be better than you were yesterday builds continual improvement and over time this ends up in you reaping the rewards.

You can build credibility and authority from promoting yourself, speaking at events, appearing on podcast interviews, writing for the HuffPost or even delivering courses to eager people wanting to learn about the industry you are in and the topic that you know most about.

There are also other ways you can build credibility, just by being seen with other experts in your field, being seen at industry events and partnering with big companies and other businesspeople who already sell their products into your ideal client base, these are simple methods which don't take too many resources.

In this modern world time can be such a problem for us to get our businesses or careers on track so making the most out of what you have is crucial to getting somewhere fast.

What have you done in the past that is remarkable?

Which companies have you worked with that are well known?

How many years have you been in your industry?

What kind of testimonials do you have to show?

Have you won any awards?

Do you teach, mentor or coach?

Who do you write for?

What people can you work with to develop skills?

Do you run any organisations that are industry recognised?

These are just some of the ideas you can use to build your statements. You can use them to begin building your credibility and of course your authority so when you speak people take notice of what you say and really absorb what you are saying.

From a personal standpoint don't talk unless you know something about the subject that is being discussed, this is a waste of everyone's time. Especially since generally a background for pretty much any subject can be found from a quick Google search or someone on YouTube…if you do make mistakes then hold your hands up and say sorry.

So now you understand the kind of things you need to put in the next section of your brand story board take the time to craft a few statements that explain what you do in the shortest number of words.

Grammar is not something to think about when putting these statements together, you can always flesh these out later when required, the main thing is having the core essence.

EXAMPLES

Awarded LinkedIn Power profile award

Delivered hundreds of brand marketing courses

Delivered workshops for IBM & Microsoft

10 Years in customer service

Pioneered a new approach to do customer architecture

Arranged 20 high profile podcast guests in month one

Written a book on personal branding □

Driven millions of visitors to your websites over the last 5 years

NOW OVER TO YOU

List 5 Authority And Credibility Building Statements

Ok so now you have the most credible statements you need to make sure that anyone can understand them, if people struggle to understand what you mean then you need to change the words. If no one knows the company or the award that you have won, then change it for another one.

I also recommend you look again at the five statements in the previous chapter you will need to do this until you complete the blueprint, once they just sound right and become a part of you then make a note on the last page of the book and your brand story board is complete for now.

Trust yourself: but still get a second opinion

You should also begin to show these statements to someone who you get on well with, someone who you feel sees the brilliance in you, if you pick the wrong person to assist this process it will not help at all.

They ideally need to be eloquent and understand what you do and then perhaps look at your statements together and review other people in your industry together; this way you will get the most out of your brainstorm with them.

Chapter 6. Discovering What Makes You Different

Never forget the probability of you being born: one in $10^{2,685,000}$

As a comparison, the approximate number of atoms in the known universe is 10^{80}

Does this not make you feel unique?

Does this not give you a great feeling of self-worth?

Just knowing that you are entirely unique must build the knowledge that you are here for a reason!

But why?

What have you done in the past that makes you unique?

What do you do that is different than the norm?

You may not know right now and that is ok, but if you take the time to think you can certainly pick out some great words that will help you stand out.

Your brand is the key, your brand is what makes you different and explaining why you are unique is so much fun, using all the right words targeted towards your target market is what separates how you are perceived VS anyone else that you see as a threat to your livelihood.

If you do feel threatened by someone or a group of other people in your industry you need to seriously have a think about why.

Why do they make you feel inferior or worried?

Why do they motivate you to learn new skills, to be better or different than them?

The good news is that fear can be a great motivator and competition is not bad, I personally believe that there is more than enough for everyone to go around.

Being worried about competition could be something that spurs you on to take the most focused action that makes you the individual that you are, it could change your life, make you that person who stands up in front of your industry peers and speaks, writes that book and is seen as an expert by other influential people in your market.

Keep The Faith

Trust yourself and take the time to list some of the reasons why you are different and better, you could be more amazing than you think.

Most of the time influential people who have built their brands are just like you and me, they just spent the time putting together a plan and have stuck to it for long enough for it to work to their advantage.

Asking your friends and family what they think of you is important, asking them what they think your key assets are, asking them what words represent you is also important to the success of your brand story board.

If you are not sincere as to what you do best and who you are then the day you put your brand plan together and others read it or meet you will create distrust versus the trust that could happen if you were just honest in the first place.

EXAMPLES

Set new performance delivery standards for social media campaigns

Business led insights to deliver real tangible results

Goes out of her way to find out what the customer wants whether it is a service or a product

Very adaptable to new technology platforms

Always exceeds expectations no matter what she must do

NOW OVER TO YOU

List Five Things That Make You Different Or Better Than Anyone Else

So now you have over most of your wording in place, take the time to review these statements above and the statements from the last two chapters too. Remember you will list your statements on the last page of this book there is the brand story board document for when you have finished tweaking your words.

Meet with your friend if you can and discuss these statements. Take your time to review them and then leave them for a couple days; taking a break really helps when you are doing such creative work.

Chapter 7. Discover Your Cornerstone Words

In addition to the key statements that make up your blueprint there are "Cornerstone Words" these words are the four or five words that represent you to others, when you leave the room, these are the words that you want people to think about you, these are words that people are already thinking about you and what you represent, but don't worry they can be consciously changed.

Trust yourself: people will still like you if you are you

Taking the time to think about which words would represent the ultimate version of you is enjoyable, investing the time to brainstorm and to use a thesaurus is a really rewarding exercise.

It is not about copying anyone else's profiles and it is not about hiring someone else to write your statements, yes, they can help you by making suggestions, but 'Brand You' needs to come from you and not be just a load of words that represent the unauthentic version of you.

How you are perceived begins with words and then image

I am sure that by just reading the words below you will realise there is a difference in how people want to be perceived and actually are perceived by not only what they say about themselves in the real world, how they dress, how they smile and how they write about themselves or interact with others on social media, it is clear that when someone is genuine and they are the same as they are online as offline that their authentic true self shines through.

More and more people want to be their friend, members of the opposite sex want them, more and more people want to hire them and work with them, just because they are their authentic selves.

Living as your authentic self brings such joy that it fills your being with such a fulfilment that you are really happy and enjoy your work and just being you is enough, there is no need to have a pretence, no need to try to cover up who you are and this helps you to become truly happy and other people around you will also feel this happiness and love working with you and spending time with you.

EXAMPLES

Sincere, experienced, networked, connected, bubbly, honest, trusted, intelligent, knowledgeable, genius, focused, fit, enthusiastic, serious, loyal, fun, funny, genuine, authentic, futuristic, traditional.

NOW OVER TO YOU

List 4/5 Cornerstone Words

Now is the time to review these words, at this stage I want you to ask 10 of your friends the words that sum you up and then make a list and compare them to the words you have listed above.

If they are drastically different then I would take the time to pick some other people to ask and perhaps revisit the words that you want people to think of when you leave the room.

You can certainly position yourself based upon how you behave and of course what you say about yourself and how you look but if the words are not a true representation, then you will not feel genuine.

Taking the time to consider this really does pay dividends. You are really in control of how you look and should not under any circumstances be using the words based on what other people think of you unless you think they reflect positive characteristics of you that you want to expand upon.

You can certainly take the time to consider the words that you would like to project VS the words that are inherent in your past behaviours and give them some thought.

Branding yourself is an art and because you have subconsciously shaped who you are in the past does not mean you cannot shape how people perceive you now and into the future.

You must use caution as you should not under any circumstances be a fake.

Chapter 8. Crafting Your Image And Using Your Brand story board

So now you have put together pretty much all the key elements of your personal brand story board.

Now you need to use your common sense to analyse the words you have used and shape them towards the people who matter, it is best to spend time reviewing the words you have used and perhaps revise two or three times or perhaps five+ times to ensure you get it right.

Keep the people who matter most at top of your mind as they are the ones who are going to help you to advance your career. They could be your clients or potential clients, they could be other people in your business or perhaps H.R. or the senior leadership team, for entrepreneurs it could be people within your team or perhaps funding managers or potential clients or strategic partners.

Taking the time to really hone the words you have used

You need to be fully understood by anyone who reads them, this is the first step in building your personal brand and completing the words that are the essence of explaining 'Brand You' to the people who matter.

Some people will instinctively know what to use for each channel, they will know what to put in their Resume or your CV as they call it in England.

Now you have the wording you need to pick the most important statements for use in your social media profiles and to be in the right places elsewhere.

Of course, using short statements for social media should reflect one of the things you do for others, so people can at first glance understand exactly what you do.

Of course, if you are writing your CV or LinkedIn profile you should take the time to list all your words from your brand story board document on the back page and then ensure these statements are expanded to be more grammatically correct.

Words come first before pictures or logos always

Many are under the misguided impression that logos and headshots come first, the amount of business leaders that we speak to daily have just blindly decided to register a business name or get a series of headshots done without deciding what image they want to portray and also how they should portray their business.

They are seduced by fancy pictures and logo designers who need briefing to ensure their brand is portrayed in the right light.

Becoming visible online and offline with great photos

You need to use a photographer that has experience in taking profile shots, not a landscape photographer. Hiring a specialist is the best way to go for most things, especially finding someone who is going to show off your brand in the right light to anyone and everyone who sees it.

If you are wondering whether you can ask a friend to take your picture, I suggest you stop everything; this is not the right mindset, unless they are good at profile shots do not even dream of it, find someone with experience.

So, let us assume you have found someone good to take your profile shots, now you are going to need to brief them.

Taking the time to look at the different shots your amazing photographer has sent you and then think about the cornerstone words you have put together and think does this picture represent those words and the image I want to portray.

Before you get onto social media sites you need to take the time to decide on the profile shot that works for you and for that site.

Depending how friendly you want to be and how you want to come across within that network, many photographers will be able to depict the image you want and help you to project the right image.

I spent some time briefing my photographer explaining that looking friendly was good but confident and approachable were also two words that I wanted to come across in the photos; she gave me quite a few options that all work well for me and my business and of course the social media profiles that I decided to use them on.

Chapter 9. Social Media

Many continue blindly on social media without the knowledge of why they are there, what message they want to get across about themselves and how to craft those messages to lead to increasing opportunities for them and whichever business they are involved with.

This chapter does not go into detail on which social media channels to use or does it go into detail on which technology platforms to use, that would require a whole book to itself and as it is constantly changing by the time it was printed it would have changed.

This chapter is to give you high level advice you can use to get the most out of social media.

Planning pays dividends and saves resources

Doing social media without having a plan is a big waste of time. Having an idea of the kind of things your audience find interesting and you ideally know a lot about is a great way to build stronger relationships with them.

You can attract great people to you, business partners, friends, romantic partners, clients and even suppliers by using social media, so keeping it professional and showing yourself off in the right light is key.

Audit your social media profiles first

Firstly, before you start sharing on social media, I would recommend you take the time to audit your online property; which platforms are you on and how do they serve you, you may find that you have some old accounts that have your old job description or an old profile picture or content that reflects badly on you.

I am not going to talk about which platforms to use as they change all the time. I do however recommend that if you want to learn more about the social media channels and tools that you email me, and I will point you in the right direction of some resources.
nat@natschooler.com

Trust yourself: you are more likeable than you think

Be authentic, be helpful, share relevant content and if you wouldn't say it to your friend's mum then probably don't say it on social media, remember all it takes is one screenshot and you could end up being fired or having to delete your account and hide from people.

Take the time to list all the taboo words and subjects

I would take some time to think about the kind of words and topics that are off limits, for example if you want to turn off your audience just talk about politics, half of them could become alienated because of your views.

Take some time to think about what you believe and how you could potentially cost yourself money by sharing the wrong things.

If you make a list of those taboo subjects and topics and of course words and use common sense, then this will pay dividends.

Make a list of the topics that you should talk about

Include seasonal topics, local topics, world topics, industry topics, hobbies, things that happened on this day etc.

Make a list of the kind of people you should engage with

I would recommend you take the time to think about who would be helpful to to engage with.

It would be best if you were thinking about local groups industry groups. There will be other influential individuals or businesses that perhaps may not be in your industry. Still, they sell to or engage with perfect people with who you are looking to mix with and develop relationships so you can work together to expand your reach to the people who matter the most.

Sharing corporate and owner generated content can be overdone

If you are sharing your companies' content or your own content be mindful that it can damage your reputation and it can stop people from following you or in fact noticing you, I recommend you take the time to think about what sort of content you are sharing and which platforms as they are usually different in terms of how many times to share content etc.

Some experts recommend 10% of your total content should be work related but personally I think it depends on how broad the topics are and whether people are interested; if you take the time to experiment it pays dividends.

Personally, I think anywhere from 10% - 30% is acceptable but like I said it depends on which platforms you are curating it to.

Scheduling content at the right time is important and there are many tools that can help you to do this.

There are also lots of tools that can help you to find people talking about the subjects you have expertise in, I will always recommend using a social listening tool if your budget allows for it.

You should always listen before you attempt to get involved in any conversation, a little like a cocktail party, walking in with a microphone and shouting is probably not a good idea there either.

Chapter 10. Marketing Yourself

Building your personal brand whichever route you choose will enable you to build your authority, credibility and gravitas in the eyes of your peers, it will mean you can share your insights and valuable opinions the right way.

Your way of doing things may not be that amazing to you but others will certainly notice your *'uniqueness'* and want to work with you or buy from you.

Sharing your perceptions, experiences and knowledge can be very insightful for people wanting to learn more about you and your business.

You can build your personal brand in many ways

Showcasing your knowledge is very rewarding and can benefit your self-esteem and boost your professional credentials.

Communicating your expertise to your peers and marketplace will reap big rewards, whether you are looking for a promotion or looking to grow your business taking the time to show off who you are pays dividends.

There are many ways to show off brand you

Marketing is a huge subject but in essence it is very simple, you want to have an audience, if you don't have one then that is not a problem you can just leverage an existing audience.

If you imagine renting some space on a billboard then that is the same as leveraging someone else's email list or social media followers.

Of course, the audience must be relevant to your topics of interest.

You can begin by commenting on other people's articles or blogs, you can also comment on other people's posts or do webinars.

These are just some of the ways you can show off your skills to the people who matter the most, do not worry too much if you don't have lots of time, just allocate about 15-30 mins a day to keeping up to speed with the latest industry and world news, it is good to stay informed and use this knowledge to engage and inform others.

Consistency is key and being authentic, if you are true to yourself and provide value and assistance to others you will succeed in building the personal brand and life that you have designed versus something you blindly inherited from your own past behaviours.

These are just some of the things you can do to market your brand

Easy to do	Not so easy	Harder to do
Like comments	Curate and comment	Public speaking
Engage in conversations	Write blogs	Host webinars
Curate content	Appear on webinars	Guest blog
Grow networks	Appear on podcasts	Host events
Introduce people	Engage thoughtleaders	Do podcasts
Attend relevant events	Share testimonials	Write books
Comment on blogs	Share awards	Deliver workshops

There are many other ways to use social proof to build your credibility. You can ask an expert in your field to recommend you, you can get a celebrity to endorse you, a user of your product or service, a large group of people endorse you and of course you can obtain certification from an industry body.

Building your personal brand is something that you need to continue to do, it is not something you do once and just leave on the shelf it is something you do every day to generate positive P.R. for growing your career success.

If you expect to just do the wording and not to develop your skills and brand moving forwards you may end up looking back and regretting not taking the actions necessary to become all who you could have become.

The more you hone your writing skills and the ability to market the authentic you, the more chance you have of being discovered and working on more of the type of projects or in the type of roles that you enjoy the most.

Providing you can explain what you do, in a language that the people who matter the most find meaningful, you will begin to create the kind of life you don't need a vacation from.

Chapter 11. Brand Story Board Document

Congratulations you now have all the words that you need to complete your brand story board.

Combine these words and variations of them in your letters, social profiles, website, press releases, magazine articles etc.

Perhaps adjust them a little on a yearly basis but do not spend your time tweaking them monthly or you will confuse anyone watching.

These words and statements can also be used, within your Resume or CV (which is more common the U.K.) and don't forget, do not rush to get it right.

Taking the time to perfect your wording, is well worth the investment and if you get stuck you should certainly take the time to use a Thesaurus.

This method has been adapted from the process that was handed down to me from my friend and mentor Douglas Commaille who used this with many brands, both people and businesses over the years, it has taken me 10 years to make it my own and now features as part of our service offering.

If you would like some assistance, then please email me nat@natschooler.com

List 3-5 Benefit Led Statements About What You Do For Others

List 3-5 Authority And Credibility Building Statements

List 3-5 Things That Make You Different Or Better Than Anyone Else

List 4/5 Cornerstone Words (*Private to you, use them sparingly, variations can be used)

Chapter 12 - Create Your Perfect Day (Bonus resource)

Imagine you could have the perfect day, every day. What would it look like? How would you feel? What would you do?

Now, imagine that you can create that perfect day without any limitations. You can put whatever you want on your agenda and make it happen. How great would that be?

In the next few pages, we're going to explore how to create your perfect day and what it might look like. I'll also give you the framework as a bonus resource to help get you started! So, whether you're looking for ways to boost your productivity or just want a little inspiration, keep reading!

The process outlined in the next few pages has dramatically helped many people to create the lives that they want to live. The steps that I followed about four years ago have enabled me to write this book and to create the life that I want to live.

What does it feel like to have designed the life you want to live?

I'm guessing you're feeling surprisingly good. You've got a career that lights you up, friends who make your heart smile and loved ones who are always ready with a supportive hug when things get tough.

Your home is comfortable and inviting, filled with all the things that remind you of what's important in life. The world feels full of possibility because nothing is off limits - not even your wildest dreams!

You've taken time for yourself and now I would love to help you take some time to create your perfect day.

Designing your perfect day can be an incredibly rewarding experience. It's about knowing what truly matters most in your life and then taking steps towards making it happen, it is pointless to try to "manifest" your life without doing anything.

Have you ever thought about what your perfect day would look like?

What do you imagine when you think of the life that's waiting for you on the other side of today?

How does it make you feel to have designed the life you want to live?

This method is a quick guide to help coaches and their clients through designing their own perfect days.

This process was originally found in Jonathan Chase's Book, listed in the resources section, he borrowed it from Frank Kern.

It certainly works and is something that I do every January to setup the new year in a positive light.

You'll be able to find out how this process can provide insights into what you want, what is important in your life, and what matters most - now and in the future.

"It's time to stop feeling stuck. You're not alone if you feel like something is missing from your life. It could be that the career path you took isn't fulfilling, or that relationships have been strained, or maybe there are just too many things on your plate, and it feels impossible to keep up."

Do not worry this is the beginning of creating the life you want to live. You are in the driving seat and beware it is not an immediate change and some of the things you probably already have in your life.

Start at the beginning.

Where:

My home is amazing, it looks like this, I have a great coffee machine, etc...

Where are you waking up?

I am waking up in a beautifully comfortable bed, the view out of the window is...

What:

What happens when you lift your head off the pillow?

What are you doing?

I go to the coffee machine and make the most amazing coffee...

Why:

Why am I doing these things?

How does it make you feel?

It makes me feel amazing.

I manage to love what I am doing every day.

This is where you put my "I believe statements."

For an example: "I believe that everyone on this planet deserves to be able to break free from worry and misfortune."

Result:

How does it make you feel?

One Last Thing

One last thing, if you enjoyed this book I would greatly appreciate it if you gave it a review.

Do feel free to reachout to me any time on nat@natscholer.com

ABOUT THE AUTHOR

Nathaniel Schooler is a Futuristic Podcast
Host, Entrepreneur & Trusted Advisor. A
renowned expert in Branding & Strategy For
Career & Business Success and podcasting
aficionado with 250+ Interviews and
collaborations with Michael Tobin OBE,
Kim-Adele Randall, Stanley Tucci and other
luminaries. Nat believes that people need to
be empowered to create their own success
by overcoming obstacles and designing their
lives for personal or business success.

Nathaniel Schooler is Chief Operating Officer - Legacy Media Hub -
Your Brand, Your Vision, Your Story - Leaving A Legacy

The Legacy Media Hub is a trusted, global incubator of hands-on
resources and tools that help you become awesome at growing your
business. He co-founded the first International Imposter Syndrome
Awareness Day with colleagues Kim-Adele Randall and Lisa
Ventura. His clients include IBM, Google, Microsoft, Oracle and
Brother Printers and he is a LinkedIn Power Profile Award winner.

Visit his website for more information on him www.natschooler.com

Resources

Grab The Brand story board Template Here
https://natschooler.com/you

If you are reading the physical book then visit:

www.LegacyMediaHub.com and search for the resources below

How To Define Your Personal Brand For Success

The Ultimate Guide To Personal Branding To Win

What Is Your Story? Brand Or Fail?

Personal Branding When Working For A Corporation

Ultimate Guide To Goal Setting To Ensure 100 % Success

11 Reasons To Use Your Own Domain Name

I also recommend these books:

Be Like Amazon – Bryan Eisenberg

Start With Why – Simon Sinek

How to Make Friends With YourSelf And Influence People – Jonathan Chase

The Journey to a Personal Brand 1st Edition – Douglas Commaille

Printed in Great Britain
by Amazon

78233438R00047